of
Wonders

Peter Scothern

New Wine Press

New Wine Press
PO Box 17
Chichester
England PO20 6YB

ISBN: 1 903725 00 3

Also included:

God's Special Miracles
Introducing Divine Healing
Deliverance from Fear
Holy Ghost and Fire
Seven Steps to New Life
How to Be 100% Ready for Christ's Return

Typeset by CRB Associates, Reepham, Norfolk.
Printed in England by Clays Ltd, St Ives plc.

Contents

Foreword

I have known the ministry of Peter Scothern for many years and thank God for his tireless service and encouragement to the body of Christ, and his steadfastness in preaching the gospel and believing the biblical promise of miraculous signs following such preaching.

The subject of this book may surprise some Christians. It will be best to take our thoughts right back to the beginning of the Christian era and to the ministry of the Lord Jesus Himself, who, although sometimes hindered by local unbelief, was otherwise able to heal all the sick who came to Him. His command to the church included the laying on of hands for the sick. The church obeyed Him into the post-apostolic era and far beyond. Augustine, concerned to understand why miracles took place at some places, but not at others, never questioned, however, that they did take place!

As the centuries went by and the word of God was not available to the people, an authoritarian religious system fell into the evils of superstition. The reaction of the Reformation was to disbelieve the reality of all miracles, including healings, and to abandon the practice of the Lord Jesus and the early church, although miraculous events continued to occur wherever faith was exercised for them. The emphasis was generally on the salvation of the soul and on the sanctification of the believer.

During the last 100 years there has been a great change, as recovery of the understanding and appropriation of the Holy Spirit have led to Christians all over the world exercising faith for divine healing, in accordance with scriptural practices. Peter Scothern's ministry in the UK and many countries overseas has been further extended in recent years through the sending of anointed prayer cloths, in accordance with Acts 19:11–12.

The Bible is full of the unexpected – God using unusual things and startling acts to draw attention to His living power and His anointed ministries and gifts. Consider the bones of Elisha which gave life to the dead, Elijah's mantle, Samson's use of the jawbone of an ass to slay a thousand Philistines, Aaron's rod which budded and Moses' rod with its miraculous powers. Elisha used a handful of meal to restore contaminated soup. His faith also caused an axe-head to swim, after he had thrown a stick into the water. Why should we be surprised at God drawing attention to His power in the unusual way He is now doing, concerned as He is to meet the increasing needs of sorrowing humanity, through faith in Jesus Christ?

Ann Whitaker, MA (Oxon.)
Pastor, Tremore Christian Fellowship
Tremore Manor, Bodmin, Cornwall, PL30 5JT
February 2001

Chapter 1

Wonder Working Power

Satan and the hosts of darkness could have trembled as the blood of Jesus stained the cross at Calvary. Satan's seeming triumph turned to doom as the true character of the blood of Christ was revealed. Maybe its chemistry and colour identified with human blood but its content was certainly omnipotent and divine. I'm sure that is why the hymn writer penned the following inspired words,

> 'There's wonder working power in the blood of the Lamb.'

Many years previously, during Israel's slavery in Egypt, the Lord God of Abraham instructed them to take the following steps. They were to select a **male** lamb without blemish or deformity and sacrifice it within their homes during the evening of the 14th day. The blood was to be sprinkled on the lintel and doorposts of the homes. This guaranteed their complete protection from the midnight curse when death angels killed the firstborn of man and beast.

So effective was the applied blood of the pascal lamb that even the most powerful evil could not cross the bloodline.

Against all evil

This being so, how much more powerful and protective is the shed blood of God's Lamb, our Lord Jesus Christ. Applied by faith it is the most effective deterrent against evil.

Let me repeat! It is not the chemistry or the colour that is so important but the actual character and life nature of the blood. Christ's sacred blood contained life (*zoe*) from heaven: eternal life, everlasting life, omnipotent life – God's life.

Because the law of sin is a spiritual force, so the divine remedy for sin must be a far superior spiritual force. God invested this superior spiritual force in the blood of His only begotten Son Jesus. When Christ shed His life blood He opened a fountain of cleansing and healing.

> 'There is a fountain filled with blood
> Drawn from Immanuel's veins;
> And sinners plunged beneath that flood
> Lose all their guilty stains.'

There is wonder working power in the blood of the Lamb. Knowing also that God remains steadfast and unchanging so the merits and the nature of Christ's blood remain as potent today as when it was first shed two thousand years ago. The precious life blood of Jesus will never, never lose its power.

God's deep respect

The Lord God's deep respect for the blood is revealed in the following statistics. The blood is the life stream of our bodies. Leviticus 17:11 states:

> *'For the life of the flesh* [body] ***is in the blood.'***

The average adult of 11–12 stone in weight has around 10 pints of blood. This contains 30 million white blood cells to help cleanse and purify the body, fight disease and carry away waste products. There are 100 trillion red blood cells to carry oxygen and food to the body to build it up, and also to keep the body at the right temperature. Other ingredients include platelets and plasma, the latter being a straw-coloured liquid comprising 55% of the blood content.

Our bodies contain 1,000 **miles** of main arteries and veins, 100,000 **miles** of blood vessels sufficient to encircle the world four times. Our hearts are the pumping station. They beat 70 times per minute, 4,200 times every hour. That is 1,000,000 times daily or 2 **billion** times in 70 years. The heart lifts 500,000 tons of blood during an average life span which equals a tanker train over 40 **miles** in length.

Essential life blood

These amazing statistics reveal to what lengths our wonderful God of creation has gone to make sure and certain our life blood circulates to every part of our body. Should the blood cease to flow for any length of time to any part of our being the affected area would wither and die. No part of our body can exist without the constant flow of life blood.

Neither can we continue in unbroken fellowship with a holy God without a continual application by faith of the blood of Jesus Christ. The blood of Jesus cleanses us from all sin. If we confess our sin God is faithful and just to forgive us and cleanse us from all unrighteousness.

They say it's old fashioned. It belongs to the old covenant. It's not for today!

Friend, it's the devil's lie. Don't you believe it. Satan hates the precious blood of Jesus. He cringes in terror at the mention of it.

An amazing confession

One day I was urgently requested to exorcise some evil spirits from a demented Indian girl. During the successful exorcism I mentioned the blood of Jesus. Immediately the tormenting spirits responded in terror, 'We hate the blood of Jesus. We hate the blood of Jesus. Torment us no more!'

During 50 years of missionary service I have personally proved more than adequate the protection of the blood of Christ. Daily I apply its divine merits to my every day experience. Travelling through the jungles of Africa, ministering to the lepers, visiting prisons and hospitals, living rough under open skies, I have valued the Divine protection the blood of Jesus affords.

Apply the blood now!

I have pleaded the merits of Jesus' blood against

sickness and disease with amazing success. I am convinced no evil force or power can cross the bloodline. When Satan has sought to attack my mind and disturb my peace I have triumphantly resisted ever fiery dart and evil thought.

I delight to sing the hymns and songs about the blood of Jesus. Also I have discovered the blessed Holy Spirit always witnesses to the blood of Christ. When the heavens seem like brass and prayer cannot penetrate, the blood of Jesus will break through the hardness and the opposition.

God will honour our faith in the blood of Jesus. We can claim the divine protection it affords. We can experience the cleansing it offers. We can confess its supremacy over all evil and the works of darkness. So apply the blood of Jesus **right now** and live in complete victory.

Chapter 2

The Priority Need of the Church and All Christians

A mighty visitation of the Holy Ghost and fire!

The present signs of the times point conclusively to the imminent return of our Lord Jesus Christ for His redeemed saints. Discerning Christians worldwide are becoming increasingly aware of this end-time truth. The priority need of the Church and all believers at this momentous hour is a powerful and personal visitation of the Holy Ghost and fire – a heaven-sent deluge of God's power and glory. I believe this is absolutely essential to enable us to respond positively to Christ's Second Advent warnings.

> *'But of that day and hour knoweth no man, no, not the angels of heaven, but my Father only. But as the days of Noe were, so shall also the coming of the Son of man be. For as in the days that were*

before the flood they were eating and drinking, marrying and giving in marriage, until the day that Noe entered into the ark, And knew not until the flood came, and took them all away; so shall also the coming of the Son of man be. Then shall two be in the field; the one shall be taken, and the other left. Two women shall be grinding at the mill; the one shall be taken, and the other left.

Watch therefore: for ye know not what hour your Lord doth come. But know this, that if the good-man of the house had known in what watch the thief would come, he would have watched, and would not have suffered his house to be broken up. Therefore be ye also ready: for in such an hour as ye think not the Son of man cometh.'

(Matthew 24:36–44)

The Second Advent parable of the ten brides-maids (virgins) further confirms the urgent need to be totally and adequately prepared for Christ's coming.

'Then shall the kingdom of heaven be likened unto ten virgins, which took their lamps, and went forth to meet the bridegroom. And five of them were wise, and five were foolish. They that were foolish took their lamps, and took no oil with them: But the wise took oil in their vessels with their lamps. While the bridegroom tarried, they all slumbered and slept. And at midnight there was a cry made, Behold, the bridegroom cometh; go ye out to meet him. Then all those virgins arose, and trimmed their lamps. And the foolish said unto the wise,

Give us of your oil; for our lamps are gone out. But the wise answered, saying, Not so; lest there be not enough for us and you: but go ye rather to them that sell, and buy for yourselves. And while they went to buy, the bridegroom came; and they that were ready went in with him to the marriage: and the door was shut. Afterward came also the other virgins, saying, Lord, Lord, open to us. But he answered and said, Verily I say unto you, I know you not. Watch therefore, for ye know neither the day nor the hour wherein the Son of man cometh.'
(Matthew 25:1–13)

Here Jesus states with absolute clarity that our lamps must be filled with oil and brightly burning at the hour of His appearing. He likens all such Christians to 'wise virgins', in stark contrast to the 'foolish virgins' whose lamps are unlit and without oil.

Oil is a scriptural symbol of the divine person of the Holy Spirit. The flame represents the sanctifying power of the Holy Ghost in conjunction with the purifying work in us of the Word of God.

The challenge of this hour demands that all believers make a serious response to John the Baptist's promise that Christ would baptize with the Holy Ghost and fire. At the dawn of the Christian era when John was baptizing in the River Jordan, he faithfully predicted the **first coming of Jesus the Messiah**. John's bold and uncompromising ministry caused intense speculation, resulting in multitudes repenting and being baptized.

Questioned by the Pharisees, John replied that he was **not** the Christ and was **not** Elijah!

> *'I am the voice of one crying in the wilderness, Make straight the way of the* [coming] *Lord . . .'*
> (John 1:19–23)

When Jesus stepped into the waters of Jordan, John proclaimed:

> *'Behold the Lamb of God, which* ***taketh away the sin of the world.'*** (John 1:29)

Also,

> *'. . . he shall baptize you with the Holy Ghost, and with fire.'* (Matthew 3:11)

This two-fold message transformed myriads of lives. Sinners were saved when Christ the Lamb of God had been crucified, and saved sinners were filled with the Holy Ghost and fire. This dual experience certainly impacted my own life. I thank God from the depth of my being for the blessedness of knowing my sins are forgiven. Furthermore, I praise Him for the baptism with the Holy Ghost and fire. Daily I seek with intense fervency to remain powerfully anointed and aflame for the glory of God.

I wonder what thoughts filled the minds of our Lord's disciples as they tarried in the Upper Room awaiting the visitation of the Holy Ghost. Was the apostle Peter still nursing painful regrets, having denied his Master three times? Was Thomas still ashamed of doubting Christ's triumphant resurrection? Were the sons of Zebedee, John and James, still smarting from Christ's stern rebuke after suggesting fire from heaven upon their opponents? Most disciples had experienced failure during Christ's ministry on earth and all had deserted Him at His arrest. They knew only too well the frailty of the flesh.

How they needed a new spiritual impetus, a dynamic heaven-sent quickening, a new surge of faith and dedication, a renewed vision and purpose. How they must have implored heaven to respond. The risen Lord heard and responded in no uncertain way. The Holy Ghost descended from heaven like a rushing, mighty wind and they were filled with the Holy Ghost and fire.

> *'And when the day of Pentecost was fully come, they were all with one accord in one place. And suddenly there came a sound from heaven as of a rushing mighty wind, and it filled all the house where they were sitting. And there appeared unto them cloven tongues like as of fire, and it sat upon each of them. And they were all filled with the Holy Ghost, and began to speak with other tongues, as the Spirit gave them utterance.'*
>
> (Acts 2:1–4)

Empowered and energised with the Holy Ghost and fire those unlearned fishermen from Galilee 'turned the world upside down'. With great power the apostles gave witness of the resurrection of the Lord Jesus. They healed the sick, cast out demons, cleansed the lepers and raised up the dead in the all-powerful Name of Jesus. They endured savage persecution with amazing resilience and patience. Tens of thousands were converted through their testimony and while those first saints of the Church remained charged and filled with the Holy Ghost and fire, they ministered triumphantly and effectively for the glory of God.

Present-day believers are in urgent need of a similar Holy Ghost and fire visitation.

Jesus predicted that during these end-time days many false prophets and teachers would arise. Sadly the present church system is defiled with distorted doctrines and false shepherds. The more emotional believers are satisfied with ecstatic experiences, bodily feelings and exciting displays. They delight in demonstrations and believe that copying the world will win the world. Many prefer head knowledge to a deep spiritual relationship with Christ. Bible truth is compromised, diluted and watered down to suit the membership.

Jesus promised that when the Spirit of Truth arrived He would guide His disciples **into all truth and show us things to come**.

> *'Howbeit when he, the Spirit of truth, is come, he will guide you into all truth: for he shall not speak of himself; but whatsoever he shall hear, that shall he speak: and he will shew you things to come.'*
>
> (John 16:13)

To be constantly filled with the Holy Ghost and fire is the divine safeguard against falling into error and being enslaved by the many false sects and shepherds operating today.

We need the Holy Ghost and fire to sanctify our lives, to rid us of the carnal dross and the self-projected lives we cling to. We need the Holy Ghost and fire to revive and restore to us the wasted years of the locust and the cankerworm.

I believe Jesus will return for a sanctified, pure and powerful company of believers. He will return for a militant and well-prepared army, flying Holy Ghost banners declaring supremacy over sin and the works of the devil.

As God took Abraham to a high mountain to view and lay claim to the promised land, so the Holy Ghost will take the redeemed sons of God to the pinnacles of divine revelation, to lay claim to their full and complete inheritance in Christ. This is our hour of golden opportunity. This is the promised time of the 'latter rain' visitation. The prophet Joel promised the former and the latter rains together. The first rain fell in the era of the Book of Acts. This was called 'the teacher rain'. We are now in the last days of God's promised 'double rain', i.e. the first and the latter rains together.

Since 1900 no less than 4,000,000 Christians have experienced the Holy Ghost baptism. Believers of varying denominations have received this life-transforming visitation from heaven. Following the 'former rain' outpouring, God changed harlots into saints, fishermen into apostles and sinners in general into sons and daughters of God. The same is happening today and I believe God will do even greater things. Unlimited spiritual resources are at the disposal of those who will pay the price and be available to Him.

Once the Holy Ghost fire has purged and purified committed Christians all things are possible. As soon as our rebellious carnal natures are consumed by the flames of the Holy Spirit, anything can happen. Once self is crucified and its remains are scorched and seared, the double rain will fill our thirsty souls.

God may have to bypass the theologians and the traditional religious groups to find a company of born-again, sanctified saints, with hearts prepared to burst into flame for the glory of God.

Now is the hour to:

> *'Blow the trumpet in Zion, sanctify a fast, call a solemn assembly.'*

Now is the time to seek the Lord with fervent intensity until the Holy Ghost and fire falls once again.

Discerning Christians can hear the midnight cry loud and clear:

> *'Behold, the bridegroom cometh!'*

Awake! Awake, saints of God! Trim your lamps! Examine your hearts! Repent of your sins! Call upon the Lord! Be baptized with the Holy Ghost and fire, allowing the divine flame to purify and sanctify your souls!

This is God's appointed hour of the midnight visitation.

Note

Audio cassette: *How to receive the Holy Ghost baptism* – available from Peter Scothern Ministries, PO Box 61, Gloucester, GL4 3AA, England. ***Send for latest tape lists.***

Chapter 3

God's Special Miracles

'And God wrought special miracles by the hands of Paul: So that from his body were brought unto the sick handkerchiefs or aprons, and the diseases departed from them, and the evil spirits went out of them.' (Acts 19:11–12)

The situation was extreme. The numbers and locations of the sick and afflicted were beyond the personal reach of the apostle Paul. So God contrived a way to bless and heal them. He inspired Paul to send handkerchiefs and aprons in the Name of Jesus. These everyday items, blessed by the Holy Spirit, became means of divine deliverance. They were used as points of contact to release the healing power of God.

Jesus had permitted the border of the garment He was wearing to be used for the same purpose. A woman with an incurable disease had touched the hem of His dress and was cured. In the land of Gennesaret a multitude of sick and suffering did likewise and were healed.

'And when the men of that place had knowledge of him, they sent out into all that country round about, and brought unto him all that were diseased; And besought him that they might only touch the hem of his garment: and as many as touched were made perfectly whole.'

(Matthew 14:35–36)

God can use any object or instrument that contributes to His purpose. Who are we to criticize or question the Lord about these matters? It pleased the Lord to use the mantle of Elijah to further His divine purpose, also the rod of Moses. Samson wielded the jaw-bone of an ass to defeat God's enemies, and Gideon fought with 'the sword of the Lord'. Jesus used a few loaves and fishes to feed two great multitudes, and water pots at Cana to perform His first miracle.

Let me repeat, God can use whoever and whatever He desires, to fulfil His will and purpose. He is sovereign in every respect. However, we must never make the mistake of magnifying the channel or the means above the Lord Himself. Our faith and confidence must always remain, steadfast and unshaken, in God. He is the instigator of these special miracles. The blessed handkerchiefs, for example, are used as a point of contact, offering a specific moment of contact for the individual to take healing from the Lord by faith and thereafter praise the results into experience.

For over 50 years I have prayerfully practised the scriptural ministry outlined in Acts 19:11–12. Requests from the sick and suffering have arrived from every corner of the world. It would be impossible for me to minister to them personally. Blessed handkerchiefs are sent without charge or payment to all sincere enquirers. Accompanying literature emphasizes as a priority the need to 'get right with God through repentance and salvation'. Those who trust and obey can be miraculously blessed. The following personal testimonies are listed for the glory of God.

- ***Leg pains disappear***
  'I born in Christian family. I am suffering with legs pain since long time. I used a lot of medicines, but I have not any results. Pastor gave me prayer cloth. Wonderfully God healed my pains. I am walking long distance without any trouble, and praising and thanking God.'
  (G. Suseela)

- ***Aids cured***
  'I am very happy to write you that when I prayed for a woman (AIDS victim) and touched her with anointed cloth, God miraculously healed her. When I visited her she was on her death-bed. Now she is healthy and active. A month has already passed. There is no symptoms of such disastrous sickness.'
  (Pastor O. Ratna Kumar)

- ***Typhoid fever cured***
  'By using the prayer cloth my daughter has been cured miraculously within three days. I am also in receipt of the tract Final Warning in Telugu. I and all the members of our family

read it and found it very good and excellent. We have decided to take baptisms.'

(N. Nageswararao)

- ***Heart disease cured***

  'K. Ramesh aged 13 years had been suffering from heart disease for seven years. He was prayed for with your anointed prayer cloth. The boy was taken for a check up by a famous heart specialist doctor who found that the disease was cured and the small hole formed in his heart was cured and no operation was needed. All the villagers wondered about this great miracle and they believed Jesus Christ as their personal Saviour and the boy's family also believed Jesus Christ as their personal Saviour.' (Pastor M. David Raju)

- ***Eye better***

  'Koti Reddy had one eye which would not work properly. I shared the Word of God with him and used your prayer cloth on his eyes. Now he is healed. Praise God. Hallelujah!

  (Rev. Manir Nadava)

- ***Heart disorder and pain gone***

  'I am an old woman with nobody to help me. I am suffering from heart attack and terrible pain that I cannot express. Pastor S. Babu came to our village preaching the gospel. Someone told him about my sickness and he came and talked to me. He brought healing prayer cloths with him and laying it on me he prayed for me. Immediately all pain is gone. All glory is to

God. The rest of my days I will live for God. Please remember me in your prayers.'

(K. Mahankalamma)

- ***Brain operation cancelled***

  'K. Basavababu was suffering from a brain tumour for the last two years. He visited all Hindu Temples but no cure of brain tumour and he was admitted to hospital in Hyderabad for operation. The doctors said "no hope". Meanwhile he heard the gospel of Christ and accepted Jesus as his personal Saviour with his family by me. I used miracle prayer cloth for his cure. He was healed by Jesus Christ. He took baptism with his family and he and his family are members in our church and worship the Lord. God did a great miracle in our brother's life and there is no need of brain tumour operation.' (Pastor M. Samson)

- ***Severe bleeding stopped***

  'I belong to Hindu family. My native village is Komminenivaripalem. From seven years I suffered severe bleeding and was too much weakness and near to death. I prayed to God and used your blessed prayer cloth. New faith came into my heart and the bleeding stopped. I praise the Lord Jesus for healing me.'

  (G. Ratnamma)

- ***Blood cancer trouble healed***

  'I was belonged to a Arya Vysya Hindu's family. Pastor A. Nava Bharatha Rao put in my body blessed miracle prayer cloth. He prayed in Jesus Name. I am healed giving glory to Jesus. Praise the Lord.' (M. Subba Rao)

- ***Leprosy healed***
  'I was attacked by leprosy. I was very sick in mind and body. Through prayer and a blessed prayer cloth I am healed giving glory in Christ Jesus Name.' (Ramakoteswara Rao)

- ***Deaf man hears***
  'I live in Krosuru Village. My hearing was greatly impaired. Through your blessed miracle prayer cloth I heard God's voice. Now I am completely healed by Jesus Name.'
  (G. Vandanam)

- ***Pain in limbs gone***
  'I was in much pain in both my arms and legs and could not walk properly. Pastor A. Navabharatha Rao brought me your God blessed prayer cloth and my pain was gone. It vanished within five days. I thank Jesus with all my heart. I am praise the Lord.'
  (Krishna Babu)

- ***Diabetic ailment and weakness healed***
  'I am suffering from five years with sugar trouble and body sickness. Through your blessed prayer cloth I am completely healed by Jesus Name. Praise the Lord.' (K. Moses)

- ***Fever cured***
  'I was struck down with fever. Pastor A.N.B. Rao put your prayer cloth on my body. He prayed

in the precious name of our Lord Jesus Christ. God came into my heart. The fever is gone and my health has been restored.'

(G. Mariamma)

- ***Cancer, snake bite, malaria fever, paralysis, polio, dumbness***
  A letter from Pastor B. Jeevaratnam in Nagulapalem, Andhra Pradesh, speaks of wonderful healings from all these afflictions. Some of the testimonies he gives are accompanied by photographs. An anointed prayer cloth was used in each case.

Testimonies I have received from elsewhere include:

- ***Recurring sickness***
  'I want to tell you how much I feel happy since I received the prayer cloth. In my heart I believe that I will be completely healed. Today it is five months, I have not been sick and that never happen for years. Normally I am very sick every two or three months . . . I am reborn. I want to be better and help other people.'

  (Monique Lucas, a Belgian lady living in Charleston, USA)

- ***Arthritis healed***
  'I received the prayer cloth . . . It has helped me with my arthritis in both hips. I feel great. No more pain. I walk five days a week. As I am 70 years old, I thank God for my health.'

  (Edith Holder, Amityville, NY, USA)

- ***Kidney function restored***

  'My doctor diagnosed me with renal failure and said I had to undergo a renal biopsy the next day to decide the amount of damage and how to proceed. My twin sister brought me the cloth, placed it over the kidneys and prayed. The next morning I had numerous vials of blood drawn to check renal function and to prepare me for the biopsy. The doctor came in and had a confused look on his face and said: "I can't understand these lab results. I had them re-run twice and they all came back that your kidneys are normal. I cancelled the biopsy. You're kidneys have excellent function and I can't understand or explain this. I was ready to put you on dialysis today." I thought, "Praise Jesus. Thank you!" I got very tearful!'

  (Mrs Rita Bednarczyk, Plymouth, MN, USA)

- ***Eyesight returning***

  'Several months ago my mother-in-law wrote to you requesting a prayer cloth for her Aunt Gerardina who went blind literally overnight. We received the prayer cloth and my mother-in-law gave it to her. Thank you. This is the follow-up letter you requested. It brings us great joy to tell you that our prayers have been answered and a miracle has occurred! Many have been praying for Aunt Gerardina, and her eyesight has been returning gradually. What I didn't know was that she had been blind in her left eye for 20 years before she completely lost her eyesight. Her doctor recently gave her an eye exam and discovered that not only is her vision returning in her right eye, but she can also see with her left eye as well! She is now able to see colors and with the help of special lenses she can read and watch television. I'm told that her doctor wants her to read to exercise her eyes. She wanted a Bible to read. He has helped her find a Bible written in Italian with large letters which she currently has on order. We continue to pray for her continued healing and give thanks to God for His blessings.' (Michele MacDonald, Boonton Twp., NJ, USA)

- ***Back problem healed***
  'My wife Lesley wrote and requested a prayer hanky from you. The back problem is now fully healed and the prayer hanky has been passed on to someone with the same type of problem. I used the hanky for a week. I carried it in my pocket all day and slept on it during the night. The results were quick and gratefully received. The Lord is good and looks after us very well.' (John Hall, Gwynedd, Wales)

Chapter 4

Small Is Great with God!

- Do you feel overshadowed by those whose talents and abilities outshine yours?
- Do you feel inferior when others take the limelight and you have so little to offer?
- Do you feel like quitting because your effort and contribution seems so inadequate?
- Take heart, Christian, small is great with God.
- Despise not the day of small things.
- He who sees the sparrow fall and takes the little child to His knee will never despise the day of small things.

Small can be beautiful

- When Jesus desired to feed five thousand hungry souls He was delighted when a small boy offered his tiny loaves and fishes.
- Jesus drew attention to the widow woman placing her mite in the offering box.

- In the Book of Revelation Jesus referred to the small and great – placing the small before the great.
- Jesus told us that the very hairs on our heads are carefully numbered.
- Small is beautiful with the Lord.
- Small is great with God.
- Take heart, child of God, your contribution to His cause, however small, is profoundly appreciated.
- A cup of cold water gifted in the Name of the Lord will be remembered and rewarded.

Your small prayer

- Your small prayer, weak effort or seemingly insignificant service is precious to the Lord.
- Take heart, child of God, small is great with God.
- Some Christians are attracted to large gatherings and assemblies. Jesus promised His presence among the twos and threes.
- Some follow big names and big ministries. God can take up the foolish of this world to confound the wise, and the weak to overcome the strong.
- He used little David to overcome the giant Goliath.
- David in turn used a small stone to accomplish the deed.

A little child

- Jesus used a little child to propound the truth of conversion and He compared faith with a tiny mustard seed.
- God who is omnipotent and mighty is also mindful of the smallest of His creatures.
- In the Old Testament He speaks of the ant, the cony and the spider.
- God is concerned about every detail in your life.
- He is not too big or too busy to care about you.
- A sick Christian failed to request prayer because she thought her problem was too insignificant for the Lord.
- A young Christian failed to pray during the prayer meeting because he could not pray fluently like other brethren.

Feed My lambs

- Another Christian lady would not give her testimony because she felt it wasn't as exciting as others.
- Remember how Jesus commissioned Peter to feed His lambs before feeding His sheep.
- Child of God, small is great with the Lord.
- Your contribution is precious to God however insignificant it may seem.

And never forget ... God prefers quality before quantity

- He is as interested in the ant as much as the elephant – the small as well as the great.
- So cast off your inferiority complex and despise not the day of small things.
- Small is beautiful with God.

Chapter 5

Deliverance from Fear

A report which recently appeared in a medical journal stated that there are no less than 5,000 classified fears. These include fears of darkness, of death, of cancer, and many diseases and sicknesses etc. During my personal ministry I have interviewed many of the Lord's people who have been subjected to tormenting fears.

The Bible declares:

> *'For God hath not given unto us the spirit of fear, but of power, and of love, and of a sound mind.'*
>
> (2 Timothy 1:7)

As I believe this verse to be of great importance, I am going to re-quote it:

> ***'For God hath not** given unto us the spirit of fear, but of **power**, and of **love**, and of a **sound mind**.'*

Fear is as old as the fallen human race and can be traced back to man's original transgression in the

Garden of Eden. Adam, having disobeyed the Lord, confessed *'I was afraid, because I was naked; and I hid myself'* (Genesis 3:10). And from Adam's day until now, fallen humanity has been subject to the tormenting influences of fear.

The fearful disciples

St Mark reminds us of a fearful experience in the lives of the Lord's disciples,

> *'And straightway Jesus constrained His disciples to get into the ship and to go to the other side before unto Bethsaida, while He sent away the people. And when He had sent them away, He departed into a mountain to pray. And when even was come, the ship was in the midst of the sea, and He alone on the land. And He saw them toiling and rowing, for the wind was contrary unto them, and about the fourth watch of the night He cometh unto them, walking upon the sea, and would have passed by them. But when they saw Him walking upon the sea, they supposed that it had been a spirit and cried out. For they all saw Him, and were troubled. And He immediately talked with them, and saith unto them, Be of good cheer: It is I; be not afraid. And He went up unto them into the ship, and the wind ceased; and they were sore amazed in themselves beyond measure and wondered.'* (Mark 6:45–51)

Here is a vivid example of how the Lord's disciples, influenced by detrimental circumstances, became so fearful that they were made afraid of the very Master whom they loved. Fear can so twist the human mind, that our very thoughts become distorted. I am convinced that this is one of the reasons why the disciples failed to recognise their Saviour after He was raised from the dead.

Here the disciples perceived Jesus walking on the sea towards them, but they failed to recognise Him. Afraid of this supernatural phenomena, they suppose Him to be a ghost or a spirit. To dispel their fears Jesus came along side and said unto them, *'Be of good cheer, it is I, be not afraid.'*

Here we find the New Testament disciples sore afraid of a supernatural manifestation of their beloved Lord. So, today, many of the Lord's people are similarly fearful of Divine manifestation. Granted, one needs to be cautious when becoming involved in the deeper experiences of the Holy Spirit, but not to a point where fear becomes an obsessive obstacle.

Recently I interviewed a lady from the Church of England who was seeking a deeper experience of the Holy Spirit, but confessed that she was afraid to pray too fervently, because she was fearful of speaking with other tongues. I pointed out to her that this is a precious manifestation and confirmation of the Holy Spirit and nothing to be fearful of. She admitted that this fearful inhibition had troubled her for many years.

Some of the Lord's people are afraid of other manifestations of the Holy Spirit. In our worldwide Divine healing services many wonderful happenings have occurred. The sick and suffering have been completely overwhelmed by the healing grace of the Lord Jesus. Others have received remarkable visions and experienced varying degrees of the Holy Spirit's power. None of these Divine manifestations should give any rise to fearful reaction. One should never fear the blessed manifestations of the Holy Spirit.

The fear of disease

In conversation with a doctor recently, he informed me that many of our sicknesses and diseases are rooted in fear. In fact the fear of disease can prove more tormenting and destructive than the actual complaint itself.

During one of my missionary crusades on the continent of India. I heard an unforgettable story. It concerns 'Prince Cholera' (Cholera being that fearful epedemic which has devastated India on so many occasions). Evidently the 'Prince' was riding horse-back across India when he was stopped by one of the border guards.

> 'Where are you going, Prince Cholera?' asked the border guard.
>
> 'On business!' the Prince replied.
>
> 'And how many victims are you planning to exterminate?' questioned the border guard.
>
> Prince Cholera answered with a sneer, 'Oh, about 50,000.'

Three months passed and Prince Cholera was seen riding in the other direction. Once again he was stopped by the border guard.

> **'Prince Cholera, the last time I saw you, you** assured me that there would only be 50,000 victims. Then how can you account for the fact that no less than 100,000 died in the recent epidemic?'
>
> 'I kept my word,' snapped Prince Cholera. 'I was only responsible for the deaths of the first 50,000 souls, the other 50,000 died from fear!'

I have known of the devastating effects of the Indian Cholera epidemics and it is true that many frightened Indians would rather commit suicide than fall victims of this dreaded plague. Let me repeat, the fear of disease can be more tormenting and crippling than the complaint itself.

I have personally interviewed scores of Christians where the fear of some disease or sickness has been at the root of their trouble. Ministering in Yorkshire some time ago, I interviewed a desperately needy woman. She was of Methodist origin and obsessed with the fear of cancer. I learned that her mother and grandmother had died of this disease at a particular age. Approaching this same age, she fearfully presumed that she would also be a victim of cancer. Obsessed by this terrible fear she became sick in mind and body.

Her husband took her to see a local doctor who gave her a thorough examination and assured her that there was no need to worry. However, as soon as they departed from the doctor's surgery, the wife whispered to her husband, 'The doctor tells everyone these things to prevent people from getting afraid.' So she continued to believe that she was a cancer victim. Her husband then took her to see a specialist, and she was subjected to a series of X-rays and blood tests which proved to be negative, but once again she insisted that the specialist had not revealed the truth and that she was still suffering from cancer.

After a while, she began to lose weight, and there were indeed evidences and signs of cancer, but her husband knew that his wife was terribly deluded. It was at this point that I was asked to interview the woman. Through the revelation of the Holy Spirit I made it very clear to her that she was cruelly bound by the tormenting spirit of fear. I also pointed out that God had not given her this spirit of fear, and that if she would yield to the claims of the Lord Jesus Christ she could be delivered. This she was willing to do, and having brought her to the place of submission I was enabled to pray positively in the Name of the Lord Jesus. I 'bound' the tormenting spirit of fear and commanded it to leave, and within a few moments the tormenting spirit departed from her body and she was gloriously released. A few months later, I learnt that she was still enjoying her new found health and that none of her tormenting fears had returned.

Fearful consequences

Obsessive fears provide soil for the disease germs to take root. Such tormenting influences can result in epilepsy, paralysis, diabetes, blood pressure, digestive troubles, and similar complaints.

A neighbour friend of mine who nursed his dying brother, became so obsessed with the fear of cancer that he died exactly twelve months to the day of the very disease that had destroyed his brother.

Fear is a poison that can affect the entire human system. Fearful impulses can release shock waves which can paralyse the nerves. In fact, severe shock waves of fear can cause premature death. It is possible to literally 'die of fright'.

In Africa where the inhabitants live under the constant fear of the witch doctor, I have heard of villagers dying of fright when threatened by evil spirits. A young woman returning home late one night from a dance was attacked by a group of drunken men. Although she suffered no physical damage, a spirit of fear so gripped her that she lost her voice and became dumb for many years. I also knew of a young housewife from Bristol who was afraid to die. She would sit up all night and eventually became a chronic invalid and was pushed around in a wheelchair, although she was only thirty-three years of age.

The Bible says that *'fear hath torment'*. To torment means to harass or to worry. Fear can harm our spiritual life. It can make us afraid to praise God. It can hold us back from fully trusting the Lord with the healing of our bodies. We read in the New Testament of a servant who was so afraid that he hid his talents. Some of God's children are afraid of one another and some have allowed the gifts of the Holy Spirit to lie dormant because they have been afraid to use them.

Simon Peter triumphantly walked on the water but soon became fearful of the consequences and began to sink. There are many bi-products of fear such as shyness and self-consciousness.

Job's secret fear

One of the most intriguing stories in the Old Testament concerns the suffering of Job. Many questions have been asked. It is true that Job suffered at the hands of the devil and it is also true that God permitted this. But there is one verse that throws light on Job's suffering that *'the thing which I greatly* ***feared*** *hath come upon me.'* So even though Job eschewed evil and walked very close to the Lord, at the same time he was nursing a secret fear. One day this fear materialized and probably this was at the root of Job's suffering. Job had nursed this secret fear for a long time and instead of laying hold of God for deliverance, fear became a destructive influence.

I was ministering at a Pentecostal church recently and having preached on the subject of fear, I appealed to those in the congregation who were bound in any way to come to the front for deliverance. Over half the congregation came forward and when I questioned them about their particular fear, the majority confessed that they were afraid of other people. In fact, I discovered through personal interviews, that nine out of ten of God's people are influenced in some way by a spirit of fear. Some are afraid to completely trust God for Divine healing, while others are afraid of opinions. Some are fearful of doing the will of God and others of using the gifts of the Holy Spirit. Some are afraid to testify and witness for the Lord while some are terrified of the devil and demons. These things should not be so!

Dear friend, **God has not** given us the spirit of fear. Fear comes from the adversary. An enemy has done this! No child of God should be subject to, or bound by, a spirit of fear.

Fear can talk. Satan can often whisper his fearful suggestions into our minds. I interviewed a lady recently who was afraid that she had committed the unpardonable sin, but I pointed out to her that this was the voice of the devil. We must close our minds to every fearful suggestion from the evil one.

Promises of deliverance

The encouraging words 'Fear not' appear 366 times in the Bible. So there is one verse for every day of the year including the leap year. We can combat our fears by claiming the wonderful promises of God. In Genesis 26:24 God says, *'Fear not, I am with thee.'* The knowledge of the presence of the Lord will dispel all our fears. Practise the presence of God wherever you go. Take Jesus with you and His presence will dissolve every fearful influence. Fear cannot hold sway when Jesus is at hand. When the disciples were in terror on the Sea of Galilee, the moment Jesus entered the ship their fears were dispelled. Always remember that the Lord is at hand and His very presence will scatter all your fears.

In Genesis 15:1 the Lord says, *'Fear not I am thy shield.'* The armour bearer usually went in advance carrying the shield. Similarly, the Lord goes before us to prepare the way and therefore we should not harbour any fears about the future. The Lord has gone before us and He is our shield to protect us from all the future as well as fiery darts of the wicked one.

The prophet Isaiah reminds us, *'Fear not I have redeemed thee.'* Remember, we belong to the Lord. We are His property. We have been redeemed by His precious blood, therefore we have nothing to fear. Satan dare not trespass upon our beings if we really understand our Bible rights.

The Bible also states that *'Perfect love casteth out all fear.'* This means that if we truly trust and love the Saviour we have nothing to fear. We can trust Him with all our consequences for He knows the end from the beginning. If the perfect love of Jesus fills our hearts then every fear will evaporate.

Fear no evil

The psalmist David declares, *'I will fear no evil, thy rod and staff they comfort me.'* Our staff is the Word of God upon which we lean in times of fearful anxiety. Our rod is the Name of our Lord Jesus which casts out all our fears. It is this heavenly authority in the Name of Jesus, that gives us power over every opposing influence. So challenge the spirit of fear in the Name of Jesus and command its power to be broken once and for all.

Jesus faithfully declared, *'**Fear not** little flock, it is the Father's good pleasure to give you the Kingdom.'* Sometimes we feel lonely or in the minority and fear besets us. Jesus encourages us to **fear not**! If God be for us, who dare stand against us? The Lord is on our side. One with God has always been a majority. Praise His wonderful Name. The Lord stood by Joshua and Caleb when they were in the minority and He will remain faithful to us. We have nothing to fear when the Lord is near.

Again in the Book of Revelation chapter 2 verse 10 we are exhorted to *'fear none of these things.'* Satan has a habit of exaggerating the small things and making them appear like mountains. He delights in deceiving the Lord's people and promoting fear and anxiety. Always remember, God is still on the throne. Fear **none** of these things! The Lord has the situation in hand. He knows the end from the beginning. Trust Jesus with every detail. Refuse to be moved. Stand fast in the faithfulness of God. He will not fail us nor forsake us. Blessed be His Name.

Means of deliverance

Always remember, God hath not given us the **spirit of fear**! An enemy has done this! We must always recognise where our fears originate. We are commanded *'Resist the devil and he will flee from you.'* So we must never, never welcome or entertain fearful thoughts or suggestions. Before fear can grip our minds we must totally and completely reject every fearful suggestion. When Satan attacks the mind we must cast out every evil imagination through the power of the precious blood and the invincible Name of Jesus.

We have been given this scriptural assurance:

> *'Resist the devil and he will flee from you.'*
>
> (James 4:7)

Fear is persistant these days. God's people everywhere are experiencing severe opposition. The adversary is attacking the minds, souls and bodies of the righteous. It is a constant conflict with the powers of darkness. We must not surrender to the devil. We must not give ground to fear. God instructs us how to resist fear!

Resisting through prayer

Satan trembles when he sees the weakest saint upon his knees! Just to kneel before the Lord will frighten the enemy. Sink down on your knees, look into the face of your risen Lord and Satan will tremble. Prayer ground is **overcoming** ground!

Resisting through praise

Fear detests a praising saint. Shouts of praise brought down the walls of Jericho and opened the prison doors at Philippi. Praise the Lord at all times – with song and in prayer. While you are **praising** the Lord, Satan has no room in your mind or conversation. Praise will scatter fear and gloom and put Satan to flight.

Resisting through faith

You belong to the God of the Universe. You are redeemed! You are God's property. You are a temple of the Holy Spirit. Command Satan to leave you. Tell him that you belong to Jesus. Challenge your fears. Command fear to leave your mind and body. Resist the devil and he **will** flee from you. Don't be afraid – do it **now**!

Resisting in Jesus' Name

If the evil persists call upon the Name of Jesus. Repeat it over and over! Defy fear in **Jesus**' Name.' Bind this power in the Name of Jesus! Step out in faith in the Name of Jesus! Act your healing in the **Name of Jesus**! Do all things in **His** imcomparable Name. You **will** overcome!

Resisting through the precious blood of Jesus!

If Satan brings your past sins before you – if he repeatedly condemns you – then confess defiantly 'I am thoroughly cleansed through the blood of Jesus! The precious blood of Jesus Christ, God's Son, cleanses me from **all** sin!' Remind Satan of this glorious truth. When **God** forgives – **He forgets**. It is Satan's strategy to bring up your past sins. Refuse his accusations! Satan was a liar from the beginning. Resist with all your faith and courage and Jesus will bring you forth more than conqueror.

Resisting with the promises of God

The **Word of God** is likened unto a **sword** in the Bible. It is an attacking weapon. Jesus successfully used the **Word of God** against Satan during the forty days of temptation in the wilderness. Take up the promises of God and resist the subtle ways of the devil. In the face of all satanic opposition confess the **Word of God**. Say 'It is written!' and the enemy will flee from before you.

As soldiers of the Lord we must press through to ultimate victory. Refuse to gratify Satan by being discouraged. Resist every sin, sickness and fear in the name of the Lord and Jesus will bring you through.

Sing the songs of deliverance. Praise the Lord at all times. Refuse to be bound! Rebuke and resist every fear!

Then claim the fulness of the **Holy Spirit's power**. Be filled with the power of God. Never be satisfied with a partial anointing. Lay claim to the fulness! Live and abide under the rich anointing of God. *'Perfect love* ***casteth out all fear****.'* So pray for a baptism of Holy Love – Jesus' love! Wait before the Lord until the love of Calvary permeates you through and through. There is **no fear** in love! When you fully and completely love Jesus every fear will disappear.

Finally, keep a *sound mind!*

The mind frequently becomes the battle ground for all kinds of fearful imaginations. Fear is the devil's doorkeeper, awaiting at the portals of the mind to disturb your peace and tranquility. Think always on those things which are lovely and beautiful. Reject all fearful thoughts and replace them with positive thoughts. Have the mind of Christ Jesus. Fear is faith in reverse! It simply means believing in the negative issues rather than the positive blessings of God. So you must change your thinking. Your thoughts must at all times be positive. Fear can be overcome through our Lord Jesus Christ. You can master every fearful influence in the mighty Name of Jesus.

Request one of our anointed praver cloths for besetting fears and we will pray positively for your release and deliverance.

Meanwhile, if you are troubled by fear in any degree, do write and share your problem with me. We welcome your communication.

Never forget:

> *'**God hath not** given us the spirit of fear, but of power, and of love, and of a sound mind!'*
>
> (2 Timothy 1:7)

Note

Request my audio tapes entitled *The Precious Blood of Jesus* and *Deliverance from Fear*.

Chapter 6

Introducing Divine Healing

Divine healing is no mystery. It is not to be confused with **spirit** or **faith** healing practised by the occultists or mediums. Divine healing is simply the operation of the **Holy Spirit** upon our sick and diseased bodies. It is the **power of God** flowing through our sick beings expelling the 'spirit of infirmity' and healing the broken tissues by supernatural means. **Faith healing** suggests 'mind over matter' – 'human will-power' etc., whereas **Divine healing**, although involving our faith and will is supremely an **act**, an **operation** of the Holy Spirit.

Healing and miracles

Divine healing must not be confused with 'the **miracle**'. Healing is a process. It means 'to recover'. Some are confused about this important issue. Jesus worked many wonderful miracles and some were miracles of healing – but Divine healing is different to the 'gift of miracles' (1 Corinthians 12). Jesus healed many that were sick as well as working miracles. 'To recover' means to heal progressively. We read that the nobleman's son began to **amend** – i.e. **Divine healing**. So if you fail to experience a **miracle** don't be discouraged. **Divine healing** is often progressive (John 4:52). It is a Divine process.

Scriptural ways to receive Divine healing

There are various scriptural ways of receiving the ministry of Divine healing. If we always keep in mind that God is the healer we can confidently take any of the following Bible steps. They are designed to assist us in making contact with God's healing **grace** and **power**.

1. Laying on of hands

Jesus commissioned 'believers' in Mark 16:18 to lay hands upon the sick in His Name. The laying on of hands enables the Spirit of God to enter our sick and diseased minds and bodies by direct transmission. The Divine power expels the 'germ life' and promotes supernatural healing.

2. Anointing with oil and the prayer of faith

A ministry of healing within the Church (James 5:14). The sick **are instructed** to call the elders of the **church** and **not** the elders to call the sick. Anointing with oil symbolizes the healing action of the Holy Spirit. The **prayer of faith** is the **disease destroying** prayer – **commanding the disease to leave in Jesus' Name**. Spirits of infirmity must be expelled by faith and authority.

3. Prayer handkerchief ministry

(Acts 19:11–12). God wrought **special healing miracles by the hands of Paul** when **handkerchiefs** and **aprons** were blessed and anointed to bring healing to the sick. These articles simply acted as a contact to replace the laying on of hands. This **ministry** is available **today** because Jesus the **Author** has never changed. This ministry is no doubt for the cases who are unable to attend special healing services.

4. Intercessory prayer

Intercessory prayer is Divinely effective for healing the sick. When prayer is offered the disease should be rebuked, the case then left in the hands of the Lord and He will do the restoring. It is necessary to **pray the prayer of faith**. Remembrance of the matter afterwards should be one of gratitude and thanksgiving **in faith for progressive healing and recovery**.

Whichever instruction is obeyed it is essential that the **heart, not merely the mind**, co-operates to believe. After applying the scriptural ministry **one must firmly believe that God's Spirit is already operative within** – destroying the disease and healing the body.

5. The communion service

The emblem of the bread at the communion service betokens the **body of Christ** scourged for our diseases (1 Peter 2:24 and Matthew 8:17). It also speaks of the type of the **Passover lamb** whose body was eaten by the children of Israel as they departed from Egypt. As they obeyed this Divine instruction they were healed and strengthened by the mighty power of God. Jesus gave His back to the smiters to secure Divine healing for all who would accept this glorious truth. When we take the bread we should accept the wonderful healing life of our risen Lord.

We all grow from a tiny germ which comes from God. Cancers, tumours and many diseases grow from a tiny germ. There are **two major spiritual powers in the universe**. The evil power of a destructive **Satan** and the **loving, healing power** of a benevolent **God**. As long as **our natural** life or spirit remains in the body we continue to live. However, as soon as the human spirit departs from the body we die and the body decays and returns to dust. So it is with disease. The moment the **power of God expels** the **germ life** the disease dies and becomes inactive. As soon as the 'spirit of infirmity' leaves our bodies the disease disintegrates. This is the process of Divine healing. Most diseases are **Satan's attack upon our bodies**. Germ **life** is spiritual; the remedy must be spiritual. There is **only one spiritual power** greater than the **'spirit of infirmity', that is the power** and **anointing** of the **Holy Ghost**. (Carefully read Acts 10:38; Matthew 8:16; 2 Peter 1:3.)

The next step: Is it God's will to heal you?

Many who are sick and afflicted could be enjoying **Divine** health and healing if only they would realize **God longs to heal and deliver them**. While there exists **one** doubt in our hearts and minds about God's willingness to heal us – **we**

may not receive healing. Prayer for healing will prove unsuccessful unless we *'ask in faith, nothing wavering'* (1 John 5:14; James 1:6). Every uncertainty concerning our Lord's willingness to heal us must be settled before we pray the **prayer of faith**.

Some may ask '**How can I ascertain God's will in respect of my healing?**'

There is no better way of determining God's will than to read the **will of God** for yourself i.e. **the Old and New Testaments**. The words 'testament' and 'will' have the same meaning.

A leper came to Jesus asking if it was the Lord's will to heal him. Jesus **spoke the word** and assured him, *'I will, be thou clean.'* So we see that **God's word** confirms **His will. God's word** is the reflection of **His Divine will.**

So open your Bible and discover God's will for yourself. First, we can learn God's will from the Scriptures and then pray God's will with a positive and fervent faith.

1. **Jesus healed in Bible days** – God has no favourites providing we have been saved from our sins and desire to please God in every way (Matthew 12:15; Luke 4:40).

2. **Jesus longs to heal and bless His people** (Matthew 14:36; Luke 6:19).

3. **Jesus is the same today** – the great unchanging Divine Healer (Hebrews 13:8).

4. **Jesus told us to pray** *'Thy will be done on earth as it is in heaven.'* There is no sickness and disease in heaven.

5. There is **not one record** in the New Testament where Jesus said 'It is **not My will to heal**!'
6. God has promised to **forgive *all* our iniquities and heal *all* our diseases** (Psalm 103:3).

Read also: Matthew 8:17; 3 John 2; Mark 1:40–41; 1 John 5:14; Exodus 15:26.

If we fail to receive Divine healing from the Lord then we must find out what is preventing us from receiving His promised blessing. It is fatal to resign to some destructive disease presuming it is God's will.

Never pray 'If it be Thy will'. Where there is 'if' there is a doubt.

First **discover God's will from the Scriptures and then pray God's will in complete faith**!

The question of faith

Faith is the channel through which God operates to bless and heal us.

> *'Without faith it is impossible to please God.'*
>
> (Hebrews 11:6)

Jesus said, ***'Only** believe and all things are possible.'* In other words – **according to your faith be it unto you**! Faith is essential to healing. Unbelief will prevent God from delivering us. **We must believe**! Faith in God is **faith in God's word**. If we believe **in God** then we must believe what **God says**. The Bible is **God's say so**! Faith in **God** is **faith in God's word – God's promises** (Mark 11:22).

Genuine faith in God is a decisive act of belief. It is stepping out upon God's infallible promises. Either the **word of God is true, or it is not true.** Either **God** will do what He has promised, or He will not do it. It is a question of belief or unbelief. Faith is not a rigorous exercise of the mind, a special intellectual gift – it is simply taking **God's word at its face value and acting upon it. God cannot lie. He can be trusted.**

To most people **faith** is merely a **word or theory**. As you claim, receive and act upon these promises **God can make them life and power.**

If your **faith** seems weak and wavering then ask Jesus to give you **His Divine faith**. Claim the **faith of God** (Mark 11). Open your heart to the **faith of Jesus** (Galatians 2:20). Then say 'thank you' in childlike simplicity, rise up and **act upon the healing promises of God.**

Do not forget *the point of contact*

She said within herself, *'If I may* ***touch*** *but His clothes I shall be whole.'*

Many fail to receive healing because they do not use a point of contact. The point of contact is the physical step we take to help our believing. The Bible says that *'as many as touched Him were made whole'* (Mark 6:56). Some fail to receive healing because they do not contact God with their faith. The point of contact is the receiving point of our faith.

It sets the time and the place for expectation of recovery. It is the precise moment we take our healing by faith. It is well to record this moment. It is the starting point of our believing. The exact moment we make our initial stand upon God's promises.

We determine the **point of contact**!

To connect with God's power, complete the circuit of faith and the Lord will deliver you. 'Believe' means 'to take', 'to grasp', 'to appropriate'. Receive your healing by faith (Matthew 20:34; Mark 5:25-34).

The point of contact is the meeting ground between your limited self and your limitless God. The power of God is available for **you now**. Why wait till tomorrow when God can heal you **today**? Make your claim on God, establish your **point of contact**, i.e. **the specific moment you accept your healing and follow through.**

Write for one of our special prayer cloths (Acts 19:11–12) – place it upon your affliction – claim the blessing – record the time and reckon your healing has begun **and then . . . armed with God's promises** rise up and act upon them!

James declares, *'Faith without works* [or actions that correspond] *is dead.'* Men of faith are men of action. When your belief becomes **action** that is real **faith**. In Mark 10:52, Jesus said, ***'go thy way. Thy faith hath made thee whole.'*** **As you act God will act.**

Real faith in God is never discouraged. It thrives on a test. Persistent faith always wins. Let nothing discourage you as **you act upon God's promise**. Allow **nothing** to change your attitude towards **God's declarations**. It may require seven journeyings around Jericho or seven dips in Jordan but hold fast to God's **word**. God cannot fail you and **His word cannot fail you.**

Never never surrender to sickness or disease. **Resist it in Jesus' Name**. At the first sign or evidence **command it to leave your body**. Resist disease exactly as you would resist sin and temptation. Never allow disease one bridgehead into your body. Rebuke every symptom in the Name of the Lord and continue to do so until you are fully released. If the symptoms return resist them again. Command them to go! Resist in the Name of Jesus. Resist through the blood of Jesus. Resist with prayer and praise. Resist by quoting God's promises audibly if possible. Once you have been healed refuse to give ground to your enemy. Resist the evil and it will flee from you.

Chapter 7

Praise Brings Victory

Do you feel depressed and weighed down? Have you lost your sparkle? Do you feel miserable?

Many Christians have lost their joy; the smile has gone from their faces. It is so easy to be weighed down by the cares of this life.

- **Always remember praise brings victory!**

Praise will revive your soul and set the joybells ringing in your heart. Praising God will scatter the clouds of doom and release the sunshine of His love to your weary soul. Praise will lift you from the valley of despair to the mountain peak of joy and blessing. Start now by counting your blessings. Look around at the good things in your life. They may be few but God has not left you desolate!

Burst into song!

There is always something you can 'Praise God' for. Paul and Silas were beaten and cast into prison.

Their situation seemed hopeless. Bleeding and sore they were thrust into darkness and fastened with chains. They had every reason to feel miserable and depressed. At midnight they burst into song, singing praises to God. It meant a determined effort. Everything seemed against them but they persisted in praising God. They offered the sacrifice of praise. An earthquake shook the foundations of the prison. All the doors were thrown open and every band loosed. What a breathtaking response from heaven! Wonderful things happened! The jailor and his family were converted to Christ. Paul and Silas were given the finest hospitality. Abundant benefits were bestowed upon them. All because they refused to be discouraged and were determined to praise the Lord.

Stop worrying and start praising God!

A praising heart will always triumph. Face each crisis in life with a thousand hallelujahs. Praise your way through every impossible situation. A shout of praise toppled the walls of Jericho. Anthems of praise enabled Israel to overcome their enemies. Praise precedes the victory. First we give thanks and the victory is sure to follow. Paul says, *'thanks be to God which giveth us the victory through our Lord Jesus Christ.'* A praising heart will always triumph. The joy of the Lord is our strength. There is divine strength and energy in praise.

- Praise will fill the soul with heavenly music.
- Praise will set our hearts on fire.

- Praise will put a new smile on our faces.
- Praise will make us look radiant.

God multiplies our blessings when we praise His Name. It is good to give thanks to the Lord. Praise is comely and good for the soul. It is easy to moan and complain. Anyone can complain and criticize. There are many 'Job's comforters' around today. That is all the more reason why we should cast off the spirit of heaviness and put on the garment of praise.

Praise the answer into reality

Many of God's children spend hours praying and pleading and then go away empty-handed because they fail to praise the answer into reality. Make your requests known with thanksgiving.

- Praise the blessing of God into your soul.
- Praise will move the stubborn mountain.
- The Lord inhabits the praise of His people!

So, shake yourself, get rid of the doom and gloom.

- Put on the garment of praise and delight yourself in the Lord.
- Lift up your heart to heaven **right now** and begin to praise the Lord.
- Be determined to give thanks whatever the cost or the opposition.

- Bless the Lord with all your heart, and at all times.
- Rejoice in God and give your soul an uplift.

Now is the time to praise the Name of the Lord.

Chapter 8

Remember Who You Are

King Richard the 'Lionheart' once faced the combined armies of five European nations. Having assessed the formidable strength of his adversaries he decided to signal his troops to withdraw. His champion knight, witnessing the King's army making an orderly retreat, rode alongside the King saying, 'Sire, **remember who you are**!' The Lionheart, challenged by this declaration, promptly reversed the order and commanded the attack. Suddenly surprised by this change of tactics the opposing enemies fled the battlefield and King Richard recorded a remarkable victory.

Christians today face a strong, subtle and persistant adversary who relentlessly attacks the spirit, mind and body. He delights to harass, confuse and depress the saints of God, but Christians under such attack, '**remember who you are!**'

Remember **you are redeemed property**. You have been bought with a price. You belong to Jesus who died to save you. You are no longer a slave of Satan **but a son of the living God**. And because you are redeemed, 'blood-bought' property, Satan **has no legal right to trespass**. You would not permit a trespasser to walk into your home! Neither should you permit Satan to trample across your life! **So demand your scriptural rights.**

Command all the works of Satan out of your life in Jesus' mighty Name. Don't question, doubt or argue with your enemy; **dislodge him with a forthright command.** Expel him from every department of your life. Shut the door in his face and refuse him access. State clearly and categorically, **'No trespassers allowed under any circumstances. I am a son of God. I am redeemed property!'**

'Remember who you are!'

Remember **the God of omnipotence has entered your life and taken up residence within you. How can you fail with the great God of the universe indwelling you?**

> *'Greater is He that is in you than he that is in the world.'*
>
> *'If God be for you, who dare stand against you?'*

One with God is always a **majority, and one with God can put ten thousand to flight.**

You are a conqueror

Because God is **with you and in you**, you are a conqueror. So rise up **son of God and cast off the yoke of bondage**. You are an overcomer. Cease retreating before sin and Satan. Cease capitulating to sickness and disease. Stop surrending to worry, fear and anxiety. Reverse the order. Go on the offensive. Resist the devil and he **will flee from you.**

'Remember who you are!'

This is the hour of victory, not defeat. So join the increasing army of God's sons who are rising up and triumphantly repelling the works of darkness. **You have complete authority in Christ's name.** Total victory is **yours today** if you **'remember who you are!'**

Chapter 9

The Joy of Giving

A small boy handed five barley loaves and two fishes to Jesus. He joyfully parted with his lunch and was delighted beyond measure when Jesus miraculously ministered to the needs of five thousand hungry folk with his unselfish contribution.

Abraham's faith was tested to the limit when he offered Isaac back to God but the divine blessing which followed Abraham's giving far exceeded his expectations.

The widow woman was probably deeply embarrassed when she slipped her mite into the temple offertory but Jesus noticed and commended her sacrificial giving.

There is real joy in giving!

'It is more blessed to give than to receive,' said Jesus.

> *'**Give** and it shall be given unto you; good measure, pressed down, and shaken together, and running over, shall men give into your bosom.'* (Luke 6:38)

*'**Give** to every man that asks of thee; and of him that takes away thy goods ask them not again.'*
(Luke 6:30)

Sincere giving strikes at the very heart of selfishness. Selfishness in turn is the core of sin. Jesus gave Himself, a willing sacrifice, thus denying every vestige of selfishness. Giving is good for the soul, especially when it is costly. God has promised **giving** will be well rewarded.

Tithing is a practical way of giving according to the Old Testament order. Jacob promised his tenth having experienced the goodness of God.

Many Jamaican Christians tithe everything – income, produce, time and possessions. They are truly blessed and rewarded by the Lord.

It is indeed more blessed to give than to receive. Why not prove this yourself? First seek divine guidance as to your giving. Then be determined to give something every day of your life.

Start this very day! Right now! Ask the Lord to guide you to some needy soul and learn the blessedness of giving. Remember to give in the precious Name of Jesus. You must always give to the glory of God.

Recently I gave a poor man some provisions. He was hungry and destitute. I also testified to God's goodness in sending Jesus to save us from our sins. He received the gift and message with gratitude. Some weeks later I was preaching many miles away and to my joy the same poor man attended my service. He was neatly dressed and wearing a happy smile. He told me how that first encounter had changed his life and helped him to become a dedicated Christian. The joy which filled my heart was indescribable. God blessed me beyond measure for the giving.

Giving may hurt! It may cost you something but there is real joy in sacrificial giving. Ask God's guidance and start giving today! You will be pleasantly surprised at the results.

Chapter 10

Seven Steps to New Life

The supreme purpose for Jesus coming to this world and dying on the old rugged cross was *'to seek and to save that which was lost.'*

To be 'saved' is a most blessed spiritual state. It involves the forgiveness of all sins, a clean heart, a pure conscience and a brand new relationship with God. It also means a new life and the impartation of Christ's glory and power to the human spirit.

The Bible declares that those who become Christians become **new creatures, new persons**, old things pass away and all things become new.

With sincere desire you can take these seven steps to salvation and become a 'new-born' child of God.

Step 1: Realise you are a sinner

The reality of sin and death is indisputable.

> *'**All** have sinned and come short of the glory of God.'* (Romans 3:23)
>
> *'All we like sheep have gone astray.'* (Isaiah 53:6)

All are sinners by **nature** and by **practice**. We are all subject to jealousy, envy, fear, lust, temper, unclean habits etc. There is **no one** perfect! We are all sinners in the sight of God. Face up to this challenge solemnly and sincerely.

Step 2: Recognise you cannot save yourself

In spite of all we do we cannot rid ourselves of sin. We cannot change our sinful nature. We are enslaved by the power of sin. Our good works, religion, self-sacrifice will not remove the power of sin from our lives. We cannot save ourselves from the power or penalty of our sin. Even our good works are like filthy rags before a **thrice holy God.**

Step 3: Jesus died to save you

For this purpose Jesus died. He took upon Himself our sinful natures.

> *'Who in his own self bare our sins in His body on the cross.'* (1 Peter 2:24)

He took our sins upon Himself so that we could be saved. Jesus **bore your sins and mine** – so we can be set gloriously free. **The pure Lamb of God is the only one who could save us.**

Step 4: Repent of your sin

Face up to the sins in your life. Be honest with God. Tell Him the truth. Open your heart before Him and be sorry for your sin. Put things right, i.e. make restitution where necessary.

Step 5: Invite Christ into your heart

Christ must **be on the inside of your life**. Many believe in **Christ** but have **not received Christ**. Kneel down in prayer. Ask Jesus to cleanse all your sins away. Ask Jesus for forgiveness and a clean heart. Now invite the living Christ into your heart. Ask Jesus to take complete control of your life. Surrender to Him **now**! Believe He has heard your prayer. Thank and praise Him by faith. Thank Him for saving you.

Step 6: Register your decision for Christ

Make a note in the cover of your Bible. Register your decision for Christ. Confess to another Christian your desire to be saved and to serve the Lord. Read Romans 10:9. Never be ashamed to confess that you belong to the Lord Jesus Christ. Confessing Christ will bring joy to your heart.

Step 7: Follow the Master daily

Read your Bible daily – beginning with John's gospel. Ask God to speak to you clearly through His Word. Pray to the Lord by simply sharing your life with Him. Learn to praise and count your blessings. Join a live church or fellowship as soon as possible. Please inform me of your decision to become a Christian.

Chapter 11

How to Be 100% Ready for Christ's Return

Each passing hour brings the promised return of Jesus ever nearer. True Christians in tune with second advent realities long to be 100% ready for Christ's return.

There are conflicting theological interpretations of the believers' participation in this great event, therefore it is wise to consider ***all* the commands and instructions** Jesus gave. Remember the 'foolish virgins' were refused access into the marriage because they were **unprepared** for the late arrival of the bridegroom. Let us identify with the 'wise virgins' and be **100% prepared** for the glorious appearing of our Bridegroom from heaven.

1. **First, we must be genuine Christians**. Genuine New Testament Christians are 'saved', 'converted' and 'born-again' (John 1:12 and John 3). Good works, religious practises, or church attendance etc. do not guarantee our salvation. We must **repent** of our sin, **open**

our hearts to Christ and receive Jesus as our personal Saviour (Revelation 3:20). Jesus must purge the sin from our lives and reign supreme in our hearts. Have **you** been 'born again'? Have you received Christ into your life?

2. We must **repent**, and be **baptized** in the Name of Jesus Christ for the remission of sins, and **receive the gift of the Holy Ghost** (Acts 2:38). This threefold **Divine** commandment was delivered to the first members of the Christian church and constitutes the initial acts of obedience for **all New Testament Christians**. So having been 'saved' we must be baptized in water and receive the gift of the Holy Spirit. (Read carefully Acts chapters 8 and 9 for a comprehensive explanation of these Divine instructions.) The gift of the Holy Spirit is a separate and distinct experience to 'being saved.'

3. **We must watch** – for we know not what hour our Lord doth come (Matthew 24:42). Repeatedly Jesus warns – **Watch! Watch! Watch!** We are to be **constantly alert and awake to the reality of Christ's return**. Like a watchman on duty we are to survey the scene of time ever mindful of our Master's return. We must **not** be found sleeping or dozing at our post but always diligently prepared and ready for this great event.

4. **We must not be deceived** by false Christs and prophets (Matthew 24:24). There are many spurious teachings, false doctrines and cults in circulation. Even established Christians are

being led astray. We must refuse to surrender our spiritual fundamentals and liberties to man-made dogmas and creeds. We must flee from all earthly religious cults **to Christ Himself** and allow His **divinely inspired word of truth to guide us continually** (John 8:31, 32).

5. **We must keep ourselves unspotted from the world**. Our spiritual garments must be clean, white and unblemished (James 1:2). Those invited to the marriage feast of the **Lamb** are arrayed in **fine linen, clean and white** (Revelation 19:8). We must keep a clean account with God at all times instantly repenting of any sin or disobedience; being constantly cleansed by the blood of Jesus.

6. **We must trim our lamps** (Matthew 25:7). Lamp trimming implies a **personal** examination of our lives in the light of God's sanctifying word. We must spend time allowing the Holy Spirit to search our hearts for any hidden darkness. We must ensure that our lives are holy and constantly filled with the fresh oil of the blessed Holy Spirit. We must burn brightly, reflecting the grace and glory of God.

7. **We must work while it is day**, for the night cometh when no man can work (John 9:4). Time is a precious commodity and so we must use it wisely and carefully. While the storm clouds of judgement darken we must spend more time praying for and witnessing to the lost souls around us. Let us give ourselves whole-heartedly to Christ's service taking every

opportunity to present the message of salvation and deliverance to the lost and needy.

8. Finally we are exhorted by the Lord Jesus:

   '...when these things begin to come to pass, then ***look up****, and* ***lift up your heads****; for your redemption* [glorification] *draweth nigh.'*
   (Luke 21:28)

   The scene around is very depressing but these events were accurately predicted by the Lord Jesus in advance of His glorious return. The outlook is exceedingly dismal but **our uplook is exceedingly glorious. Jesus** ***is coming again***. Praise the Lord! Jesus also added,

   'This generation *shall not pass away, till* ***all be fulfilled.'*** (Luke 21:32)

   Now is the hour for all true Christians to **look up and lift up their heads. We must** fix our hearts and minds upon **eternal issues** as we await the arrival of God's Son from heaven and our final glorification.

It is our sincere prayer that this important message will assist you to be 100% ready for Christ's return. We have produced many other tracts and cassettes on this vital subject. If you desire more information and details please write to: **Voice of Deliverance**, PO Box 61, Gloucester GL4 3AA.

Chapter 12

These Spiritual Dangers

According to ancient writings, one of the chief causes of the antedeluvian apostacy was the illegal introduction of black magic, astrology and enchantments. The society of Noah's day experienced an abnormal obsession for psychic phenomena and subsequently became drugged with the dark practices of occultism.

As the Scriptures record:

> *'And God saw that the wickedness of man was great in the earth, and that* ***every imagination of the thoughts of his heart*** *was only evil continually.'* (Genesis 6:5)

The situation became so intolerable that the world suffered great judgement as terrible and fearful flood waters deluged the earth. Many centuries later, the Lord Jesus referred to the days of Noah when prophesying about the events of the end time.

> *'But as the days of Noah were, so shall also the coming of the Son of man be.*

For as in the days that were ***before the flood*** *they were eating and drinking, marrying and giving in marriage, until the day that Noah entered into the Ark.*

And knew not until the flood came, and took them all away: so shall the coming of the Son of man be.' (Matthew 24:37–39)

And as these are undoubtedly the last days of this dispensation, the ever increasing interest in occultism and psychic phenomena is to be expected. There is now an abundance of occult literature available covering the whole field of astrology, fortune-telling, necromancy (consulting the dead), ghosts, hauntings, spiritualism, clairvoyance, spirit and faith healing, charms, white and black magic, amulet-pacts, and the unholy blood pacts (the habit of selling one's soul to Satan). True Christians should be made fully aware of the spiritual dangers involved in the dark, deceptive practices of occultism. For such practices are not superstitious nonsense, as some suppose, but the sinister manifestation of strong and powerful forces of darkness.

Remarkable deliverance

In May 1953 a Manila newspaper published the sensational report of a young seventeen-year-old girl who was actually bitten by demons in the Bilibid prison. The *Manila Chronicle* reported:

'Police medical investigators last night failed to give a convincing explanation to the puzzling case of the girl who claimed she was attacked by demons, and who substantiated the claim with marks on her skin. At least twenty-five competent persons including Manila's chief of police, Col. Cesar Lucero, say that it is a very realistic example of a horrified woman being bitten to insanity by "invisible persons"! She displayed several bite marks all over her body, inflicted by nobody as far as the twenty-five witnesses could see. Villanueva writhed in pain, shouted and screamed in anguish whenever the "invisible demons" attacked her.'

The doctors called in to investigate this phenomena actually witnessed the appearance of the bite marks and appealed to anyone who could assist them with their investigations. It is interesting to note that a group of spiritists who tried to help failed to make any impression. Eventually, however, an anointed minister of the Gospel offered a prayer of exorcism in the all powerful Name of the Lord Jesus and the girl was completely delivered. But the awful reality of this authentic conflict proves conclusively that the manifestations of evil powers are not to be taken lightly.

Spiritualism

There is a deep longing within man to explore life beyond the grave. Instead of accepting the truth taught by the Bible and leaving these eternal issues with God, men have entered into the forbidden realm of 'spiritism.' Many mediums are indeed able to contact spirits in other realms. These are not the spirits of our deceased loved ones – but 'familiar spirits' impersonating the dead.

Necromancy (consulting the dead) is strictly forbidden by the word of God.

> *'There shall not be found among you anyone that maketh his son or his daughter to pass through the fire, or that useth the divination, or an observer of times, or an enchanter or a witch, or a charmer, or a consulter with familiar spirits, or a wizard, or* ***a necromancer*** [consulting with the dead].
>
> *For all that do these things are an abomination unto the Lord! and because of these abominations the Lord thy God doth drive them out from before thee.'* (Deuteronomy 18:10–12)

Spiritist mediums lapse into trances to make contact with familiar spirits. A lady medium who had been actively involved in these practices for over twenty years attended one of my services seeking help and deliverance. She vividly described her intimate contacts with these 'familiar spirits' and how she implicitly obeyed their commands. The spirits became 'guides' and followed her around everywhere. After twenty years she realized the error of her ways and tried to break free from the control of her 'spirit guides.' The process proved terrifying. The rejected spirits threw her to the ground, disturbed and smashed the contents of her home and nearly drove her insane. In my service she found the Lord's deliverance.

Christians unaware

Most Christians are unaware of the fact that there are various kinds of spiritualists.

First there are the 'rational spiritualists' who deny the divinity of Christ and His atoning work upon the cross. Also they refuse to accept the divine inspiration of the Scriptures and the existence of hell.

Secondly there are the so called 'Christian spiritualists' who pursue their dark practices with Christian accessories and trimmings. I have known these particular spiritualists use the *Redemption Hymnal* in their public services. Also in their 'churches' can be found statues of Christ and the Virgin Mary along with altars and crucifixes. This type of spiritualism often appeals to a discouraged religious churchgoer seeking definite spiritual experiences.

Spiritists with strong psychic powers frequently become 'mediums'. Recently a spiritist medium was gloriously delivered and converted in one of my London services.

She served as a medium for twelve years and practised the black art of materialization. She yielded herself to these evil influences without realizing the awful consequences. She could receive and give spirit messages and distinctly detect the fearful influences of the bad spirits. She testified of a visible spiritual web which surrounded her. These were called 'guides'. Eventually she realized that she was in the strong grip of evil powers and yearned for release. One day when visiting a church in her quest for deliverance a materialized spirit in the form of a man stood by her making terrible noises and pushing her around. Only as she struggled to break free did she fully realize her awful dilemma, so strong were the evil forces that bound her. She initially became involved with spiritism quite ignorant of the consequences.

Spiritualists and spiritists, irrespective of their varying beliefs, all have one thing in common – the same spirit manifestations are to be found in their meetings. God is opposed to all who dabble in these sinister practices irrespective of their other beliefs.

Spiritualist healing

Some spiritualists claim to be endowed with gifts of healing and can produce evidence to prove this. Sincere Christians may ask 'How can an evil power heal anyone?'

Satan will do almost anything and everything to draw attention to himself. If through the healing of the body he can win the worship of the soul, Satan succeeds in his endeavours. Mediums report that those who are healed express gratitude and appreciation to the spirit 'guides' involved. Satan therefore indirectly receives the glory and the worship. This kind of spiritual healing serves the subtle purpose of wooing many newcomers into the web of spiritualism. There are certain mediums who offer to cure sick animals. This has resulted in many animal lovers becoming involved in the arts of spiritism. After all, if Satan is responsible for the spirits of infirmities which attack our bodies it is an easy matter for him to order the withdrawal of the affliction in order to win the worship of the deluded soul.

It must be made very clear to the reader that the spirits involved are the disembodied offsprings of those (the Nephalim) who perished during the great deluge in Noah's day. Enoch states emphatically:[1]

> 'the *spirits* of the giants (fallen ones) afflict, oppress, destroy, attack, do battle and work destruction on the earth, and cause trouble; they take no food, and thirst and cause offences. And these *spirits* shall rise up against the children of men and against women, because they have proceeded from them –
>
> From the days of the slaughter and destruction and death of the giants [the Great Flood] from the souls of whose flesh the spirits having gone forth shall destroy –
>
> And now the giants are produced from the spirits and flesh. They shall be called evil spirits upon the earth, and on the earth shall be their dwelling.'

So the evil spirits are earthbound disembodied beings which seek to afflict and oppress and ultimately destroy those who interfere with them.

Black and white magic

Some Christians have been subtly deceived by white magic practices. Satan offers every kind of counterfeit for the real scriptural manifestations

---

[1] From R.H. Charles' Translation of Enoch.

and experiences. Charmers and healers who use white magic often operate with scriptural quotations and use Christian symbols. White magic adherents minister as angels of light (2 Corinthians 11:14). Even mature Christians can be led astray by false signs and evidences, which can be by-products of white magic.

The number 'three' plays an important part in white magic. Charming is frequently practised using three crosses. Appearances of eerie mists and strange lights and smells accompanied by psychic disorders are apparent with white magic adherents. Others can experience terrible nightmares and apparitions, and become restless and tormented. Even Christians can be deceived by false charmers seeking after strange visions and giving heed to weird voices. It is absolutely essential that all practices in operation in Christian gatherings should tally completely with the manifestations recorded in the Word of God.

Charms and enchantments

More evil than white magic is the terrible soul-destroying art of black magic. It is in black magic that enchantments and curses are made as acts of revenge and persecution. Those involved in the dark arts of black magic are called black magicians and may have sold their souls to Satan. This practice is an unholy pact and is a covenant made with the devil frequently in blood. In some European cities there are occult churches where one can only become a member by first covenanting oneself to Satan.

Black magicians use occult books in the same way as the Christians use their Bibles. Many charms are to be found in the so called Sixth and Seventh Book of Moses. Actually Moses had nothing to do with these books. The black magic occult have simply elevated Moses as their patron saint because of his victory over Pharaoh's magicians. The Sixth Book of Moses makes the following promise:

> 'To whatever person possesses this book at any time, Lucifer makes promise to help and to carry out his commands but only as long as he possesses the book.'

Some time ago I was given these occult books and experienced strange manifestations without realizing their source. The Holy Spirit showed me clearly that the books were evil and when these were destroyed the manifestations ceased.

In many homes where these and other occult books are kept psychic disorders of varying kinds can appear.

Astrology

Astrology is by no means a new development. For hundreds of years before Christ, star-gazers, diviners, sorcerers, and astrologers were in vogue. The Philistines were noted for their soothsaying and astrology. In Daniel's day when king Nebuchadnezzar desired an interpretation to a dream the astrologers and soothsayers were consulted but were unable to satisfy the king. Finally Daniel provided the interpretation having received the same directly from his God in heaven. Astrology in its more primitive form was prolific among the heathen peoples.

In the Middle Ages it waned considerably under opposition from the Church. With the Renaissance it flourished again but with the advance of reason and science it receded almost to vanishing point. However in these last few decades, probably because of the new advance of paganism, astrology flourishes again. Computers are churning out over 10,000 horoscopes monthly. Dedicated astrologers who work on a more 'scientific' basis are overworked preparing individual horoscopes for an army of enquirers. Some folk when in need of help consult an astrologer or study 'their stars' in the newspaper. Whether you read such predictions for fun or because you believe in them, it is a fact that men and women have always desired future guidance and the need for someone to tell them what to do in a given situation.

Surely it is far more sensible to trust in One who holds the key to the future, some One far more reliable than the unregenerate astrologers. Compare the unfailing predictions of the Lord Jesus with the few successes of the unsaved astrologers and I am sure you will agree, it is far better to seek the Divine counsel of God's inimitable word (the Bible) and His anointed prophets than a host of uncertain predictions.

Divine deliverance assured

God has set certain laws and boundaries across which man must not trespass. Any unlawful transgression will bring punishment and judgement in this world and the world to come. Those trying to escape are often tormented day and night, frequently losing their reasoning or even their lives. Psychology or psychiatry sometimes fails to bring release to the occult bound. Only the supreme power and anointing of the Holy Ghost can affect a permanent release. (Read Acts 16:16–18.) The Scriptures faithfully declare:

> *'For this purpose he Son of God was manifested,* ***that He might destroy the works of the devil.'***
> (1 John 3:8)

The risen Lord proclaimed, *'All power is given unto Me in heaven and on the earth!'*

Only Jesus can break every fetter. His precious blood avails today. Full deliverance from the dark chains of occultism lie in the complete committal of one's life to Christ and the effectual covering of His efficacious blood.

Note

Audio tapes: *How to Overcome, Deliverance from Fear, Mastering Demons Today.* Available from Peter Scothern Ministries, PO Box 61, Gloucester GL4 3AA, England.

Chapter 13

Jesus Breaks Every Fetter

The following **dynamic faith-building audio tapes** are available from Peter Scothern Ministries, PO Box 61, Gloucester GL4 3AA:

1. *Introduction to Divine Healing*
2. *Overcoming Stress*
3. *When Symptoms Persist*
4. *Deliverance from Depression*
5. *Victory in the Mind*
6. *When Your Faith Is Tested*
7. *How to Keep Your Healing*
8. *Don't Be Discouraged*
9. *Seven Ways to Regenerate Your Faith*
10. *All Things Are Possible with God*
11. *How to Overcome*
12. *The Trial of Your Faith*
13. *Our Weapons Are Mighty*
14. *Be Strong in the Lord*

15. *God Wants to Bless You*
16. *God's Divine Purposes*
17. *The Power of Jesus' Blood*
18. *The Born Again Experience*
19. *Seven Steps to a Miracle*
20. *Give Satan His Marching Orders*
21. *How to Touch Jesus*
22. *End Time Overcoming*
23. *Walking with Jesus*
24. *To Be Like Jesus*
25. *How God Speaks Today*
26. *Angels to the Rescue*
27. *The Real and Unreal World*
28. *Bible Numerics*
29. *How to Be Guided by the Holy Spirit*
30. *A New Creation*
31. *Join the Resistant Fighters*
32. *God's Cosmic Vision*
33. *Natalie Sings – My Lord and My King*
34. *Natalie Sings – Living Waters*
35. *Natalie Sings Again!*
36. *God Wants to Bless You*
37. *Jesus Those Missing Years. Parts 1 and 2*
38. *Your Healing Prayer*
39. *Amazing Answers to Prayer*
40. *How the Gospel Came to Britain*
41. *Miracles and Signs in Jesus' Name*
42. *Five Things Christians Must Never Forget*
43. *Genesis Chapter One*

44. *The Baptism of Holy Fire*
45. *How to Use the Name of Jesus*
46. *The Gifts of the Holy Spirit*
47. *Faith for a Miracle*
48. *Deliverance from Fear*
49. *Christ Triumphs Within*
50. *After the Book of Acts*
51. *Christ Inside Minded*
52. *Left Your First Love?*
53. *Careless Talk Costs Faith*
54. *Our Christian Heritage*
55. *You've Got Problems?*
56. *War on the Saints*
57. *Let Go and Let God!*
58. *Delays Are Not Denials*
59. *Village School Drama*
60. *Experiencing God's Power*
61. *Water Walking Miracle*
62. *Mastering Demons Today*
63. *Signed! Sealed! Settled!*
64. *God Has Chosen You*
65. *Miracle Testimonies*
66. *Miracles I Have Witnessed*
67. *Too Much Baggage*
68. *How to Be Like Jesus*